St. Teresa Beach:
Elixir for Generations

St. Teresa Beach:
Elixir for Generations

Julie Strauss Bettinger

Dogwood Hill Books
Tallahassee, Florida

Copyright © 2019 Julie Strauss Bettinger
All rights reserved.

No part of this book may be reproduced or stored in a retrieval system, or transmitted in any form or by any means, electronic, mechanical, photocopying, recording or otherwise, without express written permission from the publisher.

Published by Dogwood Hill Books, Tallahassee, Florida
www.DogwoodHillBooks.com

Production coordination by Erica Hanway, Black Tupelo Marketing

Design and Cover by Cuneo Creative

Illustrations by Mandy Newham-Cobb

Cover Image by Erica Hanway

ISBN: 978-1-7336802-1-9

First edition

Printed in the United States of America

Author's Note

This chapbook started as one of three essays in my master's thesis *(Florida State University 2009)*, "Storybook Tallahassee: Places of My Ancestry." For many years, I kept an unadorned version of "Elixir" on my website for download: no illustrations, no photos, just the story. And it seems like every summer since, I'll run into someone who has just been to St. Teresa Beach and seen a worn, photocopied version of the story at the cottage they were visiting. They always ask, "Why don't you publish it in a book?"

Well, here it is.

Part I
A Hunting Camp for the Rest of Us

Porch sleeping. That's got to be it. Being startled awake by a giant gust of Gulf air, propping up on an elbow to see shadowy crooked oaks swaying outside a wall of screened windows. Then recognizing the tap, tap, tap turn to bat-da-tap-tap-tap of rain on the thin roof of this Depression-era log cabin at the coast. After breathing in the warm, better-than-dryer-sheets air, and reaching for the old quilt crumpled at my feet, I snuggle back into my pillow for more of the same restful sleep I knew as a child.

Yeah, that's probably what I love most about St. Teresa Beach. To me, this place is made for sleeping. In fact, why don't we just erect one of those country roadway claim-to-fame signs right out on coastal Highway 98: "Welcome to St. Teresa Beach, Home of the World's Greatest Naps."

Most cottages here at the coast have community sleeping arrangements. When I was growing up, the combination of bunk beds and double occupancy ones on the porch accommodated six bodies, easy. If you were one of the late-arrivals (or uneasy about sleeping in the open air), you crashed in the middle bedroom — another four bodies. Parents were the only ones with private accommodations — back bedroom, two up. If there was a little one — and it was yours truly for many years — you got a smaller bed or crib in the folks' room.

Couches and floor pallets in the living room supersized the place. I think the sleep record is 17 — mostly teenagers.

That's one of the charms of the coast — it's a lot like camping, only without the tents. There are communal arrangements for everything. We always have mess-hall meals. Sometimes Dad would spend the better part of a morning at the griddle, serving buttermilk pancakes and Bradley's Country sausage in shifts: adults first, with a mug of Louisiana black, then teenagers — sometimes hours later.

St. Teresa has been like summer camp to our family for going on five generations. But the tradition of families visiting this three-mile strip of sand, pines, and palmettos in Northwest Florida goes back to the 1850s. And unlike too many other Florida Gulf-front properties, the area has retained its primitive flavor. You won't find any high-rise condominiums or outlet malls here. In fact, it's a 30-minute round trip to get the morning newspaper.

Some might call it the most "forgotten" part of the Forgotten Coast of

Florida. About an hour's drive south of the Capital City of Tallahassee, you'll get glimpses of a body of water through the trees. Then some odd paved strips followed by narrow, sand lanes carved between the palmettos and brush. They're marked with hand-painted signs nailed to trees or posts with surnames — Hopkins, Lewis, Proctor, Ausley, Shaw, Moor — and farther down — Camp, Pope, Hunt, and Smith.

Take your eyes off the road to program the CD changer and you've missed St. Teresa. But slow down and turn into one of those driveways and a story will unfold about this elixir for generations.

Things They Remember...

> ... Swimming for hours at mid-tide until we got dizzy. Collecting sand dollars that made your fingers turn yellow. Watching the 4th of July boat parade from the top deck and then hearing the cannon blast from the east at someone's birthday party. Building sandcastles in front of Mom and Dad's. Flying kites. Walking out on Hannon's dock to see what folks were catching.
>
> – Tricia Merchant

The Summer Club

St. Teresa Beach is a colony of sorts — a small town collection of those who have ties to "old Tallahassee." Some people see family ties to St. Teresa as exclusive, but it's not the kind of exclusivity you can buy. It's more of a gift given to you — an inheritance — which means it's unearned. It's also a place without status symbols — old fishing caps and bare feet are great equalizers. Whatever role you play "in town," whether business owner, state politician, or ne'er-do-well, is pretty much forgotten.

Nearly all of today's owners have memories of spending their summers and school breaks at the coast. Former Floridian, now Californian, Dave Cureton calls it a "generational handrail." On visits, he sees his nieces and nephew do the same things he was doing at their age — running in tide pools, water skiing, and playing in the creek. He finds solace in the tradition.

"St. Teresa is probably the most constant place in my life," relates Cathy Lee Trifiro. "I honeymooned there, potty-trained a child there, and spread my father's ashes there in the water in front of our house. I take my girls there every summer, and it's where I have my best visits with my sister, Elizabeth." Now living in Texas, Trifiro said she gets back about once a year, always in the summer, to spend time at St. Teresa. "For me it's a blessing because so much happens in the life of my family that I miss. However, from summer to summer, an aunt, uncle, cousin, or friend will walk onto the front porch of our house that we've all shared for so long, and it's like no time has passed. It gives me a sense of being connected that otherwise would be lost."

St. Teresa's story unfolds with the cottages. And they're just that — cottages. About 150 of them, a handful surviving since the late 1800s. The rest were built mostly after the second World War (1946). Nearly all belong to descendents from the original owners, save for the few family feuds that required a sale to settle.

Only two of the collection are log cabins. Ours, a one-story, was built in 1932 by then Florida Supreme Court Justice Rivers Buford. The other is a two-story we call "the Lewis Lively house." Mr. Lively made his fortune as a Coca-Cola distributor. It was built around the same time.

Entering our living room, with its 25-foot ceilings and bare log walls, newcomers often ask, "Why a log cabin?" It was a practical matter, it seems. Cypress trees were in abundance in the area and could be stripped of their bark, notched, and fit together relatively easily. Some hemp and concrete mixture was slapped between logs, a combination that, while drafty in winter, manages to keep it sturdy, even through Florida's numerous Category Four hurricanes.

Pull back the indoor-outdoor carpet and you'll see the poured concrete base that the house sits on. In the southeast corner of the room, etched in the concrete is "1932" and the name, "Mary Buford." The Justice romantically named it for his bride and even had the deed in her name.

The original owner's son, Rivers Buford II, recalls turning 5 years old in June of that year when construction began. "I well remember holding the tape measure for my father as he laid out the forms for the concrete slab. Concrete was hand-mixed and poured on the site. Extra concrete was used to form square steppingstones for the yard. Wooden roof shingles were handmade in the evening by the campfire. There was no electricity. Lighting was by oil lamp, refrigeration was by icebox, cooking was done on an oil stove and a wood stove, and water was pumped by a tall windmill in the backyard."

Another curious detail visitors seem to notice is the height of the interior beds, which little people sometimes need a boost to access. Beds were raised to catch the breeze through the wooden three-pane slider windows opening to the screened porch. The two, three-quarter size cypress wood bed frames were built in the same room where they've sat for 75 years. Three other pieces that have remained in the cottage are also originals: a massive storage chest, four feet in height and eight feet in length, and two 10-foot trestle tables regularly used to feed the masses. All would require chainsaw action to get them through a doorway.

Located in the Panhandle of the state, St. Teresa is a slice of old Florida preserved — a place where you never tire of hearing the cries of seagulls or shrieks of toddlers facing their first waves. And let me tell you, this place is *kid heaven*.

Things They Remember...

> *... Collecting Coke bottles to cash in at Wilson's general store and leaving with bubble gum, Atomic FireBalls, and Fudgesicles. We got two or three cents for the bottles. We were digging them out of ditches and under the dock. We went door-to-door to collect them. That was our running money. It was something to do.*
>
> — Catherine Strauss

There's always something to be explored, or some great adventure to be had. Like kids at summer camp, our pockets filled up quick with shells, sharks' teeth, or Indian artifacts. And the changing sea life offers a daily lesson in itself.

"What *are* those two horseshoe crabs doing?"

Our living room mantle over the floor-to-ceiling lime rock fireplace is like a trophy case to previous adventures. There's a sea turtle skull—about half the size of a human one — a porpoise skull, a skull that looks like a wild goat's head — complete with horns — and an empty tortoise shell.

On one side of the fireplace, there's a heavy wooden oxen harness, used for pulling a wagon in another era. Dangling from the loft are coconut shells. When we were growing up, they were tied to each end of a thick rope. We took turns filling them with knickknacks and hoisting them up and down in our games of make-believe.

Traditionally, groups of Southern males have disappeared to a cabin in the woods during deer season. Well, St. Teresa Beach is like a hunting camp for the rest of us, complete with fireplaces in each bedroom.

Things They Remember...

> ...I remember going crabbing with my grandfather, Alonzo Register, at night, from Hannon's dock to Turkey Point, along with several of my cousins... wearing old sneakers, carrying buckets, croaker sacks, and long-handled crab nets. Granddaddy carried the Coleman Lantern and the flounder gig. We all tried to stay close to him to protect us from the dark and from the stingrays, which he would gig and sling out to the deep. Some nights we would drag home late with sacks full of crabs (over 100) and scallops (dozens) and an occasional flounder or two. And then the next day, my grandmother Liza would sit in a rocking chair on the porch and pick crab meat.

– Frank Douglas

Caution: Kids on Board

As with the generations before us, our days at the coast were spent on the water. Boats to us were like cars. If somebody had the keys, they *ruled*.

There was one boat stunt that we couldn't wait to imitate when we became teenagers. It was called "paratrooping." The idea is to jump out of the boat while it's moving at high speed, trying to hit the water at the right angle (or suffer a bad case of red belly). It was even better when there was an audience on Wilson's dock. We'd race by as close as possible without getting tangled in fishing lines, and everyone jumped out. Everyone — except, of course, the driver. This person was stooped down, hidden from view. When we came up for air, we would all look at the seemingly driverless boat and yell at a hysterical pitch.

"I thought *you* were driving this time!"

"No, it was *your* turn to stay in the boat!"

We kept up the charade until we were convinced we had faked everybody out. Eventually, the boat returned, or we swam back to the beach for a short walk home.

As the youngest in a large family, I tagged along with my older teenage brothers and sisters as they patrolled the waterfront. One summer, some of the teens started a gang and made up initiation rites. If you were "in," they painted your big toenail fluorescent orange. Eager for acceptance, my oldest brother, his friend, and one of my sisters climbed a water tower across the bay on a dare. Sober. They were in.

As in a small town, doors at St. Teresa are rarely locked and everyone knows your daddy. And his daddy and sometimes even his daddy, too. This small colony mentality dates back to Reconstruction.

As tensions between the North and the South heated up in the mid-1800s, Tallahassee bluebloods started looking for a way to spend their summers as an alternative to "some watering places at the north." Four developers from Tallahassee — Leroy Hall, Arvah Hopkins, General Patrick Houstoun, and John Williams — went on a hunting expedition and discovered the Island of St. James.

Things They Remember...

> ... Slalom skiing, endless card games of solitaire and Go Fish, hand churned ice-cream, sandy bed sheets, watching my older sister barefoot ski, stale saltine crackers, and hearing Mary Nell saying, "Home base to Sea Hunt," on the CB Radio.
>
> – Leslie Redding

Bordered by the Ochlockonee River on the north and east sides, the Carrabelle River on the west and the Gulf of Mexico on the south, the entire island encompasses approximately 160,000 acres.

Though only an hour's drive from Tallahassee today, in those days it required two days' travel by horse and buggy. The untamed tropics the men discovered were much the same as they had been when "La Isla de San Jaume," or "The Isle of St. James," saw its first non-Native settlers in 1527 — a small delegation of Spanish who accompanied explorer Panfilo de Narvaez on his failed expedition to Florida to find the "mythical cities of gold."

> ### Things They Remember...
>
> ... Walter Bryson Sr., a Marines fighter pilot, would pass over St. Teresa on training runs. He would wave the wings, skim the treetops, and do barrel rolls . . . saying 'hey' to his family before he headed back to the base.
>
> – Dave Cureton

During the expedition, a Catholic priest, a Catalan from Spain whose motivation was to "save the souls of the heathen natives," gained permission from de Narvaez to stay with 63 followers on an island they named after the patron saint of Spain, St. James. They lived relatively peacefully among the 2,000 Apalachee Indians they encountered, until about 1608. Seventy of the Spaniard men were martyred at the hands of Indians who blamed their religious practices (extreme penances) for their diseases. Nothing is known about the 53 women and children who survived, but somehow the name of the island remained.

Indians lost rights to the land after their appetites for European goods led to large debts owed to British Loyalist John Forbes. They ceded 2.5 million acres of land to him as compensation — later called "The Forbes Purchase." It included all or the majority of what is today four coastal counties, including Franklin, where St. Teresa is located, plus major portions of four inland counties. Forbes subsequently sold to Colin Mitchell, a Cuban merchant, in 1817, but the U.S. government questioned the authenticity of documents from Spanish archives, leaving the property in legal limbo until 1835.

Once the title was cleared, Mitchell formed the Apalachicola Land Company to market the Florida coast from headquarters in New York. Still, the roving bands of Indians in the Panhandle made Florida frontier dangerous and mostly uninhabitable. Stories of the North Florida wilderness were common — it was full of bears, wolves, wildcats, and alligators. Even sea captains avoided the untamed areas of the coast, landing only when they had no other choice. Weather patterns were also unwelcoming. Nearby Apalachicola suffered repeated hurricanes: 1842, 1844, 1850, 1851, and 1856. It was an area to be avoided.

By 1855, Colin Mitchell's Apalachicola Land Company was headed for bankruptcy. The land went into receivership and portions were sold to offset debt. That's where the ancestors of today's St. Teresa entered the picture.

The original families — Hall, Hopkins, Houstoun and Williams — settled on the Gulf-side portion of St. James Island, recognizing the prime fishing and crabbing — not to mention protection — of nearby Alligator Bay. They agreed to name it after the first daughter to be born to the men, calling it "Teresa" for Arvah Hopkins' daughter, born in 1856. She was the granddaughter of Florida's sixth Governor, John Branch, who served the Territory from 1844 to 1845.

Things They Remember...

> "...The games — ping-pong, spit, checkers, backgammon, charades — anything to do while it rained. And reading really trashy novels."
>
> – Cathy Lee Trifiro

The "saint" designation was not in the original plan. Hopkins descendents speculate that the title was added to blend with neighboring saint namesakes (i.e., St. James Island, St. Marks, St. George Island, and St. Joe — now Port St. Joe), as credit to Florida's Spanish influence.

Interestingly, they chose one of the most popular saint names and one with connections to Spain. St. Teresa of Avila (Spain) is a Doctor of the Church — one of only 33 saints (and three women) to be honored with this title.

There were no bridges linking the island when it was first settled and no direct rail route, so families arrived in wagons, toting cows and flocks of hens. The day before departure from Tallahassee, fresh horses were sent to a place called "Halfway House." Families would halt the wagons, rest, and change horses. From Halfway House, they usually went to Old Field and used a ferry to cross the Ochlockonee River to Corn Landing where they continued down a winding road, barely wide enough for the wagon, with sand so deep that much of the time was spent pushing.

"It was quite a safari," said Annie Sensabaugh, the granddaughter of founder General Patrick Houstoun. But the adventure came with health benefits, they believed. And security — even during violent storms.

Referring to the "James Island Settlement," an 1874 newspaper article related, "Last season, this portion of our coast was visited by one of the severest cyclones ever known in this section. . . . While Cedar Key, St. Marks and

Apalachicola were submerged and partially washed away, St. Teresa, that bright little jewel that decorates and overlooks old ocean's heaving bosom of beauty, stood high and safely above the maddened waves."

Alluding to its elixir effects, the article went on to say that among the 100 or so visitors, "there was the most remarkable exemptions from all forms of disease," so much that the doctor's services were not needed.

"The gay and festive 'Surgeon of the Post' luxuriated in fascinating literature, while his *patients* enjoyed the health-giving bath and baked in the exhilarating breezes of the Gulf, laden with the perfumes of the gorgeous West Indies."

A little poetic license perhaps, and some might say that the writer got a little carried away when he later reported: "Aside from the . . . health, the means of enjoyment [of St. Teresa] are enormous. Boating, fishing and hunting form the chief sources . . . for the gentlemen, the two former sports being however frequently indulged by the ladies. And such hunting and fishing . . . why we have seen eight huge bucks come into 'camp' at one time! Add to this the immediate quantity of wild turkeys, ducks, brent [geese] and smaller birds and the sportsman has his cup of happiness filled to overflowing. The fishing is the finest known on the coast, and we have seen over 200 pounds of fish taken with the hook by three fishermen as the result of an hour or two's sport. We have seen upon the grouper banks nearby 900 pounds of fish caught with the hook by eight fishermen in 25 minutes. With nets, any quantity desired can be secured." Perhaps this was St. Teresa's first fish story.

Things They Remember...

> ... Everything about Easter makes me think of St. Teresa — the night before with the dyeing of eggs in a vinegar concoction; the next morning, with all the cousins piled in the living room, we'd wake up early and remember that the Easter Bunny had hidden our baskets in the middle of the night. We'd all go running around in different directions until we had our prize — chocolate bunnies, chocolate peanut butter eggs, marshmallow bunnies, all buried in a nest of pastel-colored tinsel. Then we'd head outside to search for Easter eggs (and most importantly, the golden egg ... for which Uncle Pat would give us $10).

– Sarah Jordan Redding

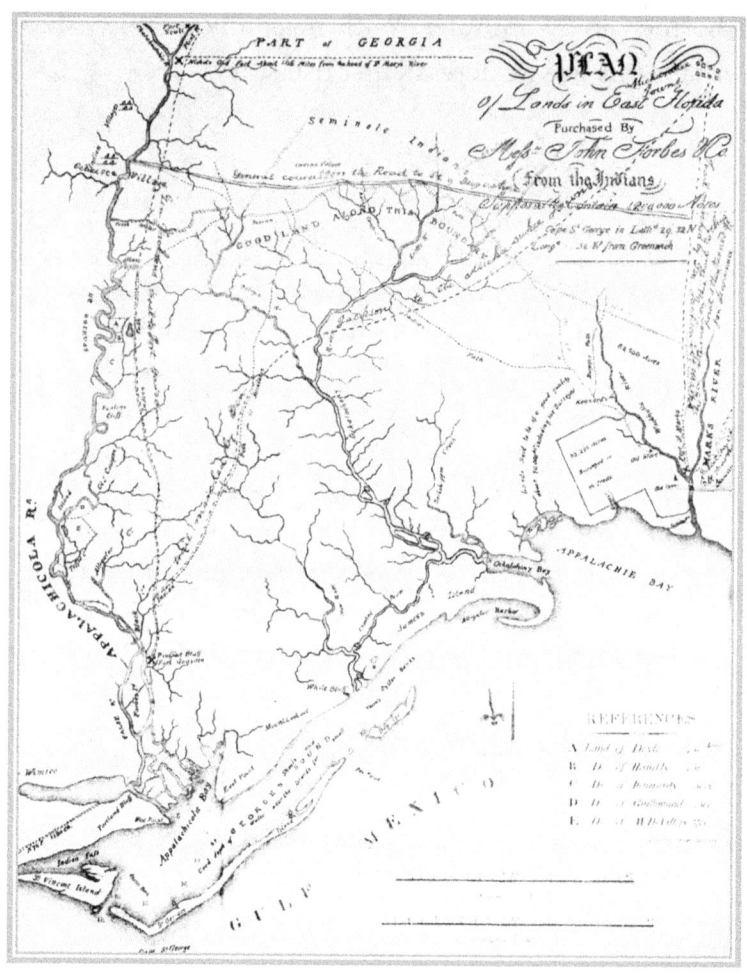

Franklin County, where St. Teresa Beach is located, was one of four coastal counties included in The Forbes Purchase. (Map circa 1817) Photo: State Archives of Florida

The original families named their coastal community after the next female to be born. That honor went to Arvah Hopkins' daughter, Teresa. She's pictured here with her brothers. Photo: State Archives of Florida

St. Teresa is where you never tire of hearing the cries of seagulls or shrieks of toddlers facing their first waves. Photo: State Archives of Florida

Every walk is full of great finds—shells, sharks' teeth and even Native American artifacts like these, discovered on the beach.

Part II
Staking Their Claim

Dr. Flavius Augustus Byrd, a Miccosukee physician, and his wife Catharine Blake Byrd built a cottage at the "new seaside resort of St. Teresa" in 1874. In a letter he wrote the summer of that year, he referenced visiting it 30 years prior, and said he expected to stay only three days. But finding an abundance of building material and available labor, he started building immediately. He finished the project in six weeks.

There were ten other houses on the island, and another 30 lots were sold. The summer population of that year grew to 130 people with "cots, lounges, benches and a part of the floor called into requisition" to accommodate those who overnighted.

Weekend visitors in that era relied on a combination of train service to St. Marks plus steamboat or sailing vessels to get to St. Teresa. The June 16, 1874 *Weekly Floridian* advertised passenger service connecting St. Marks, St. Teresa, and Apalachicola on a large sailing vessel called the Kete B. Some passengers stopped at River Sink and proceeded to the ferry on the Ochlockonee Bay, then traveled on to St. Teresa. It took an entire day, which vacationers didn't seem to mind. As one article described it, "Leaving Tallahassee at 9 a.m. after a delightful cruise, we can enjoy a chowder oyster stew or deviled crabs, prepared by loving hands, at 6 p.m."

In the late 1880s, a U.S. Mail steamboat called the Walkatomica was put in operation between St. Marks and Teresa, making trips every other day during summer months, adding to accessibility.

In 1894, families had another option. The C.T.& G. (Carrabelle, Tallahassee, and Georgia) Railroad began running from Tallahassee to Carrabelle with a stop at McIntyre (a small mill town eight miles from Teresa). Travelers then rode a wagon from the depot to the cottages through sand that often swallowed the wagon wheels.

During this early era, all the homes faced a boardwalk with a "bath house," or private swimming area for women. The Victorian times dictated that women not be seen in public dressed in bathing attire — traditionally, a two-piece gown from shoulder to knees, plus a set of trousers with leggings extending to the ankles. At night, the boardwalk became the center for social activities.

Residents made sure a doctor, preacher, and postal service were available during summer months. One family, the Bradfords, provided a teacher for summer school.

Swimming, sailing, and recreational fishing, crabbing, and scalloping took up the better part of their days. Families lived off the land with seafood as their primary fare. They brought large supplies of staples with them — meal, flour, salted meat, ham and bacon, and canned fruits and vegetables, but there was no ice for storage. Daily catches were supplemented with chicken, eggs, and fresh milk from cows.

Efforts to turn St. Teresa into more of a commercial success started in 1878 with establishment of "The Ocean House," for "people ... who have been unable to have their own cottages at St. Teresa." The home of Major Poole was renovated and became the largest building at St. Teresa with added sleep quarters at two other cottages. It was overseen by Tallahassee's City Hotel manager.

The demand was growing, however. In 1882, the Tallahassee newspaper touted "quick and reliable transit," with a disclaimer, "but one thing is needed to make it a very desirable resort for Middle Floridians, and that is a suitable hotel, kept in good style." It suggested, "some enterprising man, or a joint stock company, might find a hotel at St. Teresa a very profitable investment."

Advertisements in 1885 offered a boarding house managed by Mrs. E.W. Gamble. Rates were $35 a month ($798 in 2009 dollars), $10 a week ($228), and $1.50 a day ($34). It was operated in combination with Capt. Slusser and the steamboat Walkatomica. The venture didn't last long, however. During a storm that hit in 1899, the three-story hotel was blown off its foundation blocks. Families propped it up using big timbers on either side, until it was finally torn down sometime after 1907.

Today's beach families still refer to the parcel first settled as "Little St. Teresa"

> ### Things They Remember...
> "... chasing the 'bugman' and giving him a six pack of beer so he would give our yards 'extra' DDT (amazing that we are all still alive after running around in the toxic stuff!) ... collecting shells with our grandmother who knew the name of everything. And I remember sitting on Diehl's dock as a teenager and knowing it was time to go home when our porch lights started flashing."
>
> – Loranne Ausley

or "Old St. Teresa," which now consists of 18 cottages. Other parts developed as Perkins Beach and Cochran-Phillips Beach. But few can tell the dividing lines, except to repeat a little of the coastal community's colorful history.

St. Teresa saw a bit of industrial activity beginning in 1905 when a portion of the island — 17,000 acres — was sold by Simeon D. "Foogie" Chittenden to Frank Cochran and his partner F.M. "Dadbummit" Phillips. Cochran and Phillips used it for turpentining.

Tallahassee families were starting to acquire automobiles in the early 1900s, and the city saw its first paved streets in 1912. By 1920, autos were everywhere, though the U.S. boom in road building didn't extend to the coast. What is now an hour's drive from Tallahassee took about five hours with no paved roads, except a one-mile strip of crushed lime rock through the town of Woodville. To cross the Ochlockonee River, you relied on a hand-pulled ferry that only accommodated two cars. Ferryman Ike could be summoned by beating an old circular saw suspended from the limb of a scrub oak tree with an ax. Travelers could hear Ike's reply across the river, "I'm a comin'! I'm a comin'!" He used a cable connected to live oaks on either side of the river to propel the ferry.

When Cochran and Phillips decided to get out of the turpentining business in 1925 and sell to DuPont interests (later The St. Joe Company), they saved the beachfront portion of the island, platted it out, and sold 50-foot lots for $250 each. It was to be called Cochran-Phillips Beach.

The story goes that when George Perkins, the Cochran-Phillips attorney, traveled to New York City to close the deal with DuPont, he returned owning a portion of the beach — 50 lots, west of Old St. Teresa, called "Perkins Beach."

"I'm kin to both sides, that's why I can tell the story," said Tommy Perkins. "I used to ask my grandmother how the strip of land came to be known as Perkins Beach and she said, 'Well, if you were to ask Ida Phillips (wife of Dadbummit), George Perkins stole it.'"

In subsequent divided interests and sales, 24 lots came to be known as Cochran-Phillips Beach, 33 as East Cochran Beach, and 33 as West Cochran Beach.

The first home to be built on "new" St. Teresa (Cochran-Phillips Beach) was the Frank Cochran house, built in 1929. The Lewis Lively house, a two-story log cabin, was built next, and the Chief Justice Rivers Buford house (ours) was built in 1932.

The mid 1930s brought a building boom of sorts to St. Teresa, especially after a bridge over the Ochlockonee River was completed in 1935. However, a paved road from the bridge to St. Teresa wouldn't come until five years later. The war years improved transportation south of the Capital City to Teresa, but the east-west road to Apalachicola didn't come until 1952, when Highway 98 was extended.

After George Perkins' death in 1941, his widow sold approximately 20 acres of land with 350 feet of beachfront to Bill Wilson, just before the entire island was confiscated by the U.S. military.

Water never ages but the land surrounding it carries the scars from years gone by. Many of those scars are still visible at St. Teresa.

Bay North, low rise condominiums on the east end of Old St. Teresa, is best remembered as Camp Weed. St. Teresa was chosen by the Episcopal Diocese of Florida as one of its camping spots, following on the heels of its St. Augustine and St. Andrew's Bay/Panama City Beach locales. Started in 1924, these were all named "Camp Weed," after the late Rev. Edwin Garner Weed, the third Episcopal Bishop of Florida. By 1940, about 400 people were attending each summer.

Things They Remember...

> ...we went through Sopchoppy and always stopped for a Delaware punch. I remember going out on the dock at night for ghost stories told by one of the older kids, and it scared us to death. We — my cousin Mary Jane Marshall Butler and I — ran home on the small sidewalk terrified of something grabbing us.
>
> We did plays at night and the grownups had to watch. Betty Ann Roberts McCarty was a great actor. We made up songs and danced. Later, when I was older, there were boyfriends and walks to Wilson's dock. (We even drove a Jeep out on it.)
>
> – Grace Albritton

When the U.S. Army took over the Panama City site at the start of WWII, the St. Joe Paper Company gave the Diocese beachfront property at St. Teresa. Then the Army chose St. James Island to train troops for amphibious landings, so the camp, along with the scattering of privately-owned cottages, was seized by the government for the duration of the war.

Population on St. Teresa swelled in war time. Camp Gordon Johnston opened on St. James Island in 1942, where more than 250,000 men were trained in four separate camps sprawled 20 miles along the coast. With the rotation of entire reinforced Army Divisions, the camp population sometimes topped 30,000. It was the second largest military installation in Florida at the time.

During the Camp Gordon Johnston days, the beach cottages became married officers' quarters and homes for the top Army brass. My family's log cabin figured prominently during this period — it served as headquarters of General Holcumb, Commander of the Base.

First called Camp Carrabelle, after a nearby town, the military base was later renamed in honor of Col. Gordon Johnston (1874-1934), who served in three wars and earned many decorations, including the Congressional Medal of Honor for bravery during the Philippine Insurrection in 1906.

The west side of St. James Island, now Lanark Village retirement community, was used as the officers' quarters. Camp Gordon Johnston covered 165,000 acres and extended 36 miles along the Gulf shores. Much of the territory was left in its natural state for training purposes. Across the Bay from St. Teresa, Alligator Point served as an aerial gunnery area, and to the west, Dog and St. George islands were used to practice amphibious landings and airdrops.

The area had been selected because the bay reefs were more like those at Normandy Beach than any other in the U.S. But it was described as a "terrible camp for enlisted men, with sand floors in the barracks, stand-up-to-eat mess halls and outside latrines, all deliberately designed to prepare the troops for overseas hardships." General Omar Bradley was the most famous soldier to train at the camp.

After VJ Day (Victory Over Japan) in August 1945, the camp was the scene of a wild, continuous, and spontaneous celebration. Two years later, all U.S. military presence had vanished.

Things They Remember...

" *... Sneaking stealth-like into Camp Weed to ring the bell. We were hellions, GI Joes. You never really got what you were doing — which was waking up an entire camp full of hundreds of church kids. Although many were caught, there were never any confirmed cases of shaved heads.* "

– Catherine Strauss

In 1946, the church camp returned to the St. Teresa Beach site, which now had barracks, mess halls, and offices, easily converted into dormitories, a dining room, a chapel, a recreation house, and a crafts/hobby house. Local beach families rarely interacted with the campers or camp counselors, with one exception: sneaking into the camp at night became a rite of passage for St. Teresa teens.

In 1978, the Episcopal Church Diocesan convention found a more centrally located site (likely free of night-time harassment) and sold the St. Teresa property to developers who leveled it and built Bay North condominiums.

Another remnant of the former military site is an expansive paved area like a parking lot—originally created for military drills — which we call the parade grounds. As teenagers, we held tailgate parties there. The sandy, deserted area was one place adults would just as soon avoid, making it fair game for most teens. Grace Albritton, who started going to St. Teresa in 1935, called it "a dangerous, fun place to visit."

As it did in other parts of the U.S., Tallahassee's population boomed after the war and families started returning to St. Teresa Beach. Chief Justice Rivers Buford expressed an interest in selling his log cabin at the coast "because real estate prices would probably never be that high again," and my grandfather Alex Strauss bought it for $8,900. When he died in 1969, he left the cottage to my father, Buddy Strauss.

Things They Remember...

> *... sleeping on the front porch and being awakened by magnificent thunderstorms — lightning illuminating the entire beach. I remember discovering boiled shrimp and gin and tonics on that same front porch.*
>
> *– Frank Douglas*

For my siblings and me, St. Teresa wasn't just a two-week vacation, but lasted the entire summer long. Like earlier settlers who took their live chickens, goats, and pigs at the turn of the century, our stay-at-home mom used to pack up trunkloads of groceries (it always took two cars), along with her six kids, and headed for the coast. My father made the hour-long commute weekdays to his real estate job.

Wilson's general store had opened in 1945 and provided basic provisions, including two gas pumps, to serve the families returning to the island. It was the first and only retail establishment in the history of St. Teresa and was typical of the touristy roadhouses, announcing its souvenirs on billboards leading up to the site. Inside, you found postcards with women in '50s style bathing suits (they were still there in the '70s), big floppy beach-style hats, and a large selection of sunning products. There were shelves full of trinkets — mostly jewelry and collectibles made from Florida's native shells. And — ahhh — a freezer case full of ice cream bars, irresistible to hungry kids and their sun-soaked parents.

About a dozen free-standing efficiency apartments had been built on the property to house soldiers during the war, so Wilson's started renting them mostly to South Georgia folk. You knew someone wasn't from around here when you saw their severely sunburned flesh.

Things They Remember...

> *...I remember flirting with a fisherman's daughter, from Georgia, on Wilson's dock one night. I woke up the next day with a hickey on my neck, which I tried to hide from my mother, to no avail. I told her it was from a skiing accident. Other forbidden fruits were discovered there, too.*
>
> *– Frank Douglas*

At some point in our lives, avoiding the sun with a hat and oversized t-shirt switched to conquering it, strategically planning how to get a tan leading into spring break, right down to bronze tops above our bare feet and — the ultimate — no strap marks. It took careful planning to maintain the color up to the start of summer.

Things They Remember...

> ... I remember it was a competition to see who could take the biggest car back to Leech Lake. Steve Taff took his mother's Cadillac, Les Peterman (from Alligator Point) took his dad's Fury III, and I would never admit taking my mom's Chrysler Newport Custom back there. I would never admit taking daddy's Volvo back there either.
>
> – Rivers H. Buford, III

Initiation into St. Teresa Beach traditions always included a four-wheel drive to Leech Lake, a deserted sink hole and swimming area carved out of the St. Joe Company woods. Located across the road from the beach, it was a popular gathering spot for teens.

Ted Strauss discovered the lake as a teenager in the summer of 1968. He and his friends "borrowed" a St. Joe bulldozer and opened up a road to it. They also bulldozed one side of the lake to create a beach.

To his knowledge, the place didn't have a name until one of the girls emerged from the waters one day with a leech in tow. The name stuck.

Better than heaven?

My Aunt Isabel and her sister Lolly inherited a cottage at St. Teresa from their father, "Big Jack" Yaeger, an early owner. Through the years, Isabel has expressed her fondness for the place, telling young people, "If you're real good, when you die you go to a front porch on St. Teresa."

Our front porch at St. Teresa is where my late sister-in-law spent much of the last three years of her life, to offset the cold steel world of chemo wards and hospital rooms. When she died of plasma cell leukemia at the age of 41, my brother brought a bucket of sand from the coast to her burial. After her casket was lowered, we each grabbed a fistful and tossed it into the grave.

Comparisons to heaven are common for St. Teresa, and one Tallahassee man admitted praying about it. Dennett Rainey looked toward the sky one afternoon and said, "God, it wouldn't hurt my feelings one bit if when I get to heaven you send me right back here to St. Teresa Beach."

The heavenly or medicinal effects of St. Teresa on a person's constitution have been a constant among the generations. Even today's visitors to the coast would relate to an 1885 article citing the "Proverbs of St. Teresa, Tallahassee's sea-side resort"...

- A sniff of salt sea air in mid-summer is a tonic not to be despised.

- A plunge in the surf with the mer-maids — or with no maids at all — is the best antidote for the blues, and can even cure chills and fever.

- A sail well spread and filled with a stiff gulf breeze, with the leeward gunwale just skimming the surface of the water, is the most healthy and exhilarating stimulant one can safely indulge in [on] hot, sultry [days].

- A wind from the southwest, strong enough to "blow your hair off," laden with the coolness and freshness of the sea, keeps your lungs in good order, your liver in action and your spirits exuberant.

I would add only one thing:

a long nap at St. Teresa will give rest to your soul.

Chief Justice Rivers Buford built this cypress wood cabin in 1932, later owned by Greek immigrant Alex Strauss and his descendants.

James Cureton is said to have created this monument for his father-in-law, Alex Strauss, when a new walkway was added to the cabin in the 1950s.

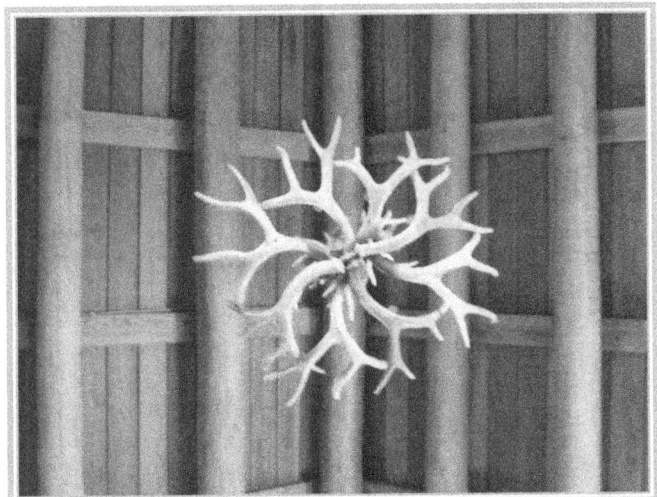

Older cottages along the beach tend to attract curious décor, a trophy case to previous adventures.
Photo: Melissa Meyer Strauss

"A plunge in the surf... is the best antidote for the blues and can even cure chills and fever." So claimed the "Proverbs of St. Teresa, Tallahassee's Sea-Side Resort" (Weekly Floridian, 1885)

Comparisons to heaven are common for the coast. Isabel Yeager Strauss was fond of saying, "If you're real good, when you die you go to a front porch on St. Teresa."

Wilson's Beach included a touristy roadhouse that offered basic provisions along with cottage rentals, a communal dock and public access to the Gulf. It closed in the mid 1970s, but still holds the record for being St. Teresa's only retail business. 1949 postcard, State Archives of Florida

The parcel that was first settled is called "Little St. Teresa" or "Old St. Teresa." It's closest to the former Camp Weed. Other parts have been known as Perkins Beach and Cochran-Phillips Beach, but few can tell the dividing lines. Photo: State Archives of Florida

Wilson's dock weathered many hurricanes but was finally toppled by Hurricane Agnes in 1972 and never re-built. Generations of memories cling to those pilings.
Photo: Erica Hanway

This is not a coastal destination that gets featured in travel magazines. It's rugged. Curly oaks and tall pines are signature St. Teresa.

Giant white squirrels remind us what a rare and special place we have at the coast.

Severe weather changes the look of the shoreline in dramatic ways. But somehow the old cottages remain sturdy, even through Category Four hurricanes.

Photo: Jennifer Boone

Water never ages but the land surrounding it carries the scars from years gone by. Many of those scars are still visible at St. Teresa.
Photo: Melissa Meyer Strauss

Hannon's Dock—like Wilson's and Diehl's—has been a popular gathering spot for generations of St. Teresa beachgoers. In the background, Alligator Point.
Photo: Dave Cureton

Sandpipers along the shoreline are fun for all to marvel over and for dogs to give chase. Photo: Erica Hanway

Dave Cureton calls St. Teresa a "generational handrail." Favorite activities are timeless: walking bare foot on the sandbar, playing in the creek and motor boating. Photo: Melissa Meyer Strauss

www.ingramcontent.com/pod-product-compliance
Lightning Source LLC
Chambersburg PA
CBHW082216090526
44584CB00025BA/3771